TRENCHES

Terry Deary
Illustrated by Martin Brown

Scholastic Canada Ltd.
Toronto New York London Auckland Sydney
Mexico City New Delhi Hong Kong Buenos Aires

To Rob Davis, brill! MB

Library and Archives Canada Cataloguing in Publication
Deary, Terry
Trenches / Terry Deary, author ; Martin Brown, illustrator.
(Horrible histories handbooks)
ISBN 978-0-545-98567-3
1. World War, 1914-1918--Trench warfare--Juvenile
literature. 2. World War, 1914-1918--Campaigns--Western
Front--Juvenile literature. I. Brown, Martin, 1959- II. Title.
III. Series: Deary, Terry. Horrible histories handbooks.
D522.7.D435 2009   j940.4'144   C2009-901161-1

First published in the UK by Scholastic Ltd, 2008.
First published in Canada by Scholastic Canada Ltd, 2009

Text copyright © Terry Deary, 2008
Cover illustration copyright © Martin Brown, 2008
Illustrations copyright © Martin Brown, Rob Davis, 2008

5 4 3 2 1   Printed in Canada   09 10 11 12 13

Mike K.

CONTENTS

INTRODUCTION 5

CONTENTS

INTRODUCTION

History can be horrible. People can do dreadful and cruel things to one another. Some even kill others and believe they are doing GOOD!

And of course.

The family he's fighting for are sometimes right behind him in his killing . . .

1. Yes, "We don't want to lose you but we think you ought to go" really were the lyrics to a popular song at the start of the First World War. It was called "Your King and Your Country Want You."

The country he's fighting for is right behind him. Well, the men giving the orders are usually a LONG way behind him, nice and safe . . .

What is our task? To make Britain a fit country for heroes to live in.[2]

The men who fought in the blood and mud of the First World War trenches were heroes. Lions. But the people who sent them into danger were the ones to blame for the bloodshed. As a Frenchman said 40 years before, in another war, "You are lions led by donkeys."

So the common soldier had to face TWO enemies . . . the soldiers on the other side AND his own leaders who were sending him into terrible danger.

What most books forget is the soldiers on BOTH sides were lions. What you need is a book that takes you into the lion's den on both sides. A soldier's handbook to help you survive the trenches.

Where will you find a book like that? Only a *Horrible Histories* Handbook will do!

2. David Lloyd George, the British Prime Minister, said this two days after the First World War ended in 1918.

PART I: BRITAIN
KNOW YOUR ENEMY

You are fighting for THE ALLIES: Britain and the British Empire, France, Belgium, Russia, Italy and Serbia (the USA, China, Greece, Portugal, Japan and Romania will join in later).

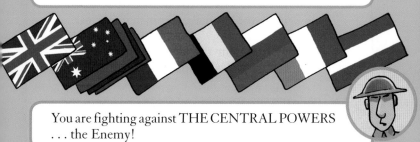

You are fighting against THE CENTRAL POWERS . . . the Enemy!

4 August 1914. The German army has marched through Belgium to attack France, so Britain has joined the war to help "Poor Little Belgium." Here are five "facts" that are being spread about the War. They may not be true . . . but believe them anyway. Learn to hate!

1. In Belgium British nurses are being carved with knives and left to die in burning hospitals. And German soldiers have been throwing babies up in the air, catching them on bayonets, roasting them and eating them.

2. Don't trust our friends the French. Apparently the French are charging us rent to live in the trenches in France!

3. Don't trust our own businessmen. They're selling British cement to Germany to build German defences and British wool to make German uniforms!

4. Germans are taking the fat off their corpses to make explosives.

5. The Germans are short of soldiers. They're not German soldiers you can see in the trenches, they are dummies stuffed with corpses and straw.

Of course one of the deadliest fellers is the one who plans the battles and sends you to fight them. Your OWN leader!

PUBLIC ENEMY NUMBER 1

Field Marshal Sir Douglas Haig

Job: Leader of the British Army

Nickname: The Butcher of the Somme (because he sends so many Brit soldiers to their death at the Battle of the Somme in 1916).

Peculiarity: He says, "I am all for using aeroplanes and tanks, but the main thing is the man and the horse. I feel that as time goes on you will find just as much use for the horse as you ever have in the past." (Horses don't stop machine-gun bullets like a tank does, but never mind. Haig also says machine guns are not such great weapons!)

Weakness: He goes to visit wounded soldiers in hospital. It upsets him so much his friends tell him to stop visiting the army hospitals. So he does. The soldiers then think Haig doesn't care.

Nasty streak: Thousands of men die when he sends them to march against machine guns. He doesn't stop the attacks. He tells the British people they just have to get used to seeing their men slaughtered: "The nation must be taught to bear losses."

Most likely to say: "The way to capture machine guns is by grit and determination."

Least likely to say: "The way to capture machine guns is with me marching by your side!"

CURIOUS CLOTHING

You are given a uniform for fighting but you need to know about some of the more unusual clothing.

THE TEDDY BEAR
Army jerkin made from goatskin. It is given out in winter 1914 when the troops get cold — but not as cold as the goat that lost its skin.

NECKLET
A silk-lined collar which is supposed to stop a large, speeding bullet taking your head off.

THE BRITISH WARM
An overcoat, knee-length and tight at the waist. Cozy, but it's only for troops on horseback . . . and officers, of course.

THE BRODIE A British steel helmet, invented in February 1916 for snipers — ace shooters who hide and take pot shots at the enemy. Some officers have started to buy them for themselves. The shape is just like the ones worn by English archers at the Battle of Agincourt . . . and that was in 1415. John L. Brodie invented the 1916 one.

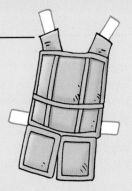

BODY ARMOUR The Dayfield is perhaps the best known. It is made from steel plates sewn into a cloth shirt and usually worn under the army uniform. It is expensive — usually officers can afford it, not the ordinary soldiers.

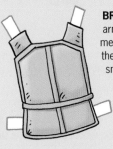

BRITISH ARMY ARMOUR The army's own armour has curved metal plates for the chest and the back. It is meant to stop snipers' bullets. But the metal is very thin, and curves in toward the middle, so any bullet hitting in the centre of the armour will be sent into you, not away from you!

BULLET-PROOF BIBLES
Pocket-sized copies of the New Testament have suddenly sold in tens of thousands. They are being bought by worried British mothers for their sons. There are stories of bullets being stopped by these little Bibles. There may be one or two true cases of Bibles stopping "spent" rifle bullets. They are not a lot of good against high-explosive shells and machine-gun bullets. Still it's good to have God on your side . . . or your front.

TIGHTS

Many Scottish soldiers wear kilts. When the Germans send over clouds of poison mustard gas, the gas goes up the kilts and burns their bums. Many Scottish soldiers have started wearing ladies' tights to save their . . . skin.

ER... JUST THE TIGHTS, BOB

GRUESOME GAS

A new First World War danger is from gas attack. To stop choking you need to put on a gas mask. But what if you don't have a gas mask handy?

Die horribly? No, there is hope for you.

Orders from army chiefs say . . .

If you are caught in a gas attack without a gas helmet then:

1. TAKE OUT YOUR HANDKERCHIEF

2. URINATE INTO THE MATERIAL TILL IT IS SOAKED

3. TIE IT ROUND YOUR MOUTH AND NOSE AND BREATHE THROUGH IT

The orders don't say what you should do if you don't feel like taking a pee at the time!

BARMY BATTLE PLANS

The hardest fighting is done by the foot soldiers — the infantry. They call themselves the PBI . . . the Poor Bloody Infantry.

The British dig trenches in the ground so they are safe from enemy bullets and can attack.
The enemy sit in their trenches to defend.

The French and British build simple trenches because they don't plan to stay there. They are always wanting to attack. The Germans build solid and clever trenches. They use concrete and have dugouts deep underground.

BRITS ATTACK ACROSS THE BIT IN BETWEEN — WE CALL THAT "NO MAN'S LAND!"

GERMAN TRENCHES

Of course the Germans will be firing shells and machine-gun bullets at them as they march across "no man's land."

The Germans also put up barbed wire to slow down the British attacks. The Brit generals have a way to help the PBI . . .

FIRSTLY WE FIRE SHELLS TO SMASH THE BARBED WIRE. A STREAM OF SHELLS IS CALLED A BARRAGE

BARBED WIRE

THEN WE SEND SHELLS TO DRIVE THE GERMANS OUT OF THE TRENCHES AND MACHINE-GUN POSTS

RETREATING GERMANS

AS YOU MARCH ACROSS NO MAN'S LAND, WE SEND SHELLS AHEAD OF YOU TO KEEP THE ENEMY HEADS DOWN. WE CALL THIS A CREEPING BARRAGE

DOWNED HEADS

Mines

British soldiers in the trenches do a spot of mining. No, they are not looking for coal. Here's what they do . . .

1. They dig a long tunnel under no man's land till they are under the enemy trenches

2. They pack the tunnel end with explosives and run wires back to the British side

3. When they are ready to attack, they set off the bomb. The Germans are too shattered to stop them

Great idea! Except most Germans learn to stay well back behind the trenches. The Brits blow up the mine and this becomes a signal to the Germans . . .

BOOM

THE BRITS ARE ABOUT TO ATTACK! BACK TO YOUR MACHINE GUNS

The explosion is just like a very large alarm clock for the Germans.

Prisoner plans

Not every Brit soldier is sporting. You are supposed to take prisoners if an enemy soldier surrenders. Not every officer wants to be bothered with looking after prisoners. One says . . .

And, by the way — no prisoners. If any of you come back here to me with prisoners, you'll be in for it. We're not taking any more prisoners and the enemy knows it. Shoot the beggars. If you bring 'em to me, I'll shoot them — and you too.

WICKED WEAPONS

If you are going into battle you will need to carry a lot of stuff. The army gives you weapons (usually a bayonet and a rifle) but many soldiers use extra special ones too . . .

BAYONET

A long knife fastened to the end of your rifle. Used to stab the enemy to death when you haven't time to fire. Invented in France in the 1600s.
For: Good for toasting bread, opening cans, scraping mud off uniforms, poking a trench fire or digging toilet pits.
Against: You can have someone's eye out if you're not careful. And if you stick it in the enemy you may have trouble pulling it out again!

KNUCKLEDUSTERS

Wrap these around your fingers.
For: If you are hand-to-hand with a German soldier, and you have run out of bullets, these will help you smash his teeth in or put out his eyes . . . if he doesn't get you first!
Against: Another heavy thing to carry and not much good if your enemy still has a loaded gun.

MAXIM MACHINE GUN

A gun that fires off a stream of bullets, around ten bullets every second.

For: One machine gun is said to be worth around 80 rifles. Good for defending your trench.

Against: The Maxim weighs 62 kg and needs to rest on a stand. It gets hot very quickly and bullets can jam. The British army is not keen on them in 1914 and only have a few hundred. The Germans have 12,000 at the start of the War and 100,000 by the end.

🏴‍☠️ DID YOU KNOW…? 🏴‍☠️
Soldiers use wooden clubs (like cave-men) and metal maces (like knights in armour), as well as all sorts of short knives.

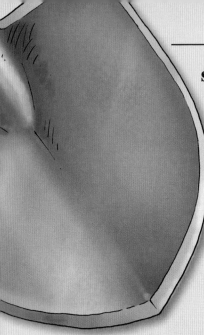

SHARP SPADE

Many soldiers use a short-handled spade (or "entrenching tool") fastened to their bayonet.

For: You can sharpen the blade so that it's just as deadly as a bayonet. These tools could then be used to "dig in" after soldiers had taken a trench.

Against: Very clumsy to carry. It can trip you up or get caught in the barbed wire.

HAND GRENADE

Hand grenades are bombs you can throw – but in the First World War they can be deadly ... for the thrower! There are accidents every day.

For: They are thrown by hand . . .

Against: . . . but you can only throw them about 30 metres. At 30 metres your enemy can shoot you. Oh, dear. So some soldiers invent grenades with handles. The hair brush (or racket) grenade was a paddle-shaped piece of wood with a tin box fastened to it. Steel plates in the box are flung out when it explodes and rip into enemy bodies and faces.

It's a bit hard to get the throwing right. Some soldiers have catapults. Elastic Y-shaped ones (like they used at school).

A sports shop in London, Gamages, makes one that fires grenades 150 metres. Sadly the rubber soon goes rotten. If it snaps as you let go, the grenade lands at your feet. Oooops!

SPRING GUN

Captain West invents the spring gun. It is a cross between the Roman balista and the medieval French trebuchet.

For: Can throw bombs up to 250 metres. It's still as dangerous as the hand-held ones.

Against: It has to be carried through the trenches by two men and if it fails then the bomb drops at your own feet.

CRICKET BALL GRENADE

A little bomb like a cricket ball with a handle. Strike the ball like a match then throw it.

For: Some other grenades explode at your feet if you drop them, but not this one. The Germans aren't very good at cricket so they can't bat it back.

Against: If the ball or the box get wet they won't work. If you can't throw a cricket ball you're not much use throwing this!

TERRIBLE TOILETS

There are no proper toilets in most of the Brit trenches, just buckets. If you upset the sergeant then you may be given the job of taking the buckets out after dark. Your job is to dig a hole and empty the buckets.

Perilous pee

Once you are out of the cover of the trenches you are in danger, of course.

But some soldiers still light cigarettes to hide the smell from the buckets. Enemy snipers are just waiting to aim at the glow of a cigarette end.

EMPTYING TOILET BUCKETS CAN BE BAD FOR YOUR HEALTH

PING!!

HAVING A POO CAN BE BAD FOR YOUR HEALTH

Even going to the toilet shed just behind the trenches can be dangerous. The enemy know men use these toilets at dawn and like to drop a few shells among the toilet huts to catch the soldiers with their pants down!

Bucket and chuck it

In the 1917 battles in Flanders the troops do not have proper trenches, just shell holes and sandbags. There are no toilet huts. One officer writes home . . .

If you want to do your daily job of urinating and otherwise there is an empty tin can, and you have to do that in front of all your men, and then chuck the contents (but not the tin can) out over the back.

He forgot to say one important thing. Find out which way the wind is blowing first!

🏴‍☠️ DID YOU KNOW . . . ? 🏴‍☠️

Army boots have to be tough. The trouble is the leather can be so hard it gives your feet blisters. Old soldiers know the answer . . .

YOU NEED SWEET PEA MIXTURE

WHAT'S THAT?

PEE IN THE BOOTS, LAD, AND LEAVE THEM OVERNIGHT!

You probably want to try this. Just remember to empty your boots before you put them back on!

FOUL FOOD

Welcome to tea in the trenches. It may not taste the same as the tea you get at home. A soldier's water has chloride of lime added to kill the germs. The trouble is the lime makes the water taste terrible, even when it is boiled.

It's a bit like drinking water from your local swimming pool.

Rotten rations
Every Brit soldier gets this food each day . . .

DAILY RATION 1914

1 1/4lb (565g) meat

4oz (110g) of bacon

BEEF

3oz (85g) cheese

1 1/4lb (565g) bread

5/8oz (18g) tea

4oz (110g) of jam

1/2oz (14g) salt

1/36oz pepper

3oz (85g) sugar

1/20oz (12 mustard

8oz (225g) fresh vegetables

1/2 gill rum

1/4oz (7g) tobacco

YUMMY

Horrible hotpot
British soldiers have to eat a terrible-tasting tinned stew called
Maconochie. A joke recipe appeared in a soldiers' newspaper.
Sadly it is close to the truth!

MACONOCHIE HOTPOT

1 Open one tin of Maconochie rations.

2 Warm gently until the greasy oil floats to the
top. Remove this by blotting it up with a piece
of flannel. (Place this to one side for later use.)

3 Remove the black lumps from the tin. These
are potatoes.

4 Squeeze the greasy oil from the flannel into
a frying pan and gently fry the potatoes.

5 Take two handfuls of dried vegetables (they
look like any other dead leaves). Mix with
water flavoured with chloride of lime and pat
into a pancake. This should be gently fried
after the potatoes.

6 Heat up the remains of the stew, then serve
with the potatoes and vegetables on a cold
enamel plate.

Soldiers are also given bully beef (like corned beef) to which they like to add raw onions. Sometimes they have to eat this with hard biscuits.

Some young soldiers complain about their food. Ernest Parker (10th Battalion, The Durham Light Infantry) says:

Army food was monotonous and in the trenches bully beef and bread, often without butter or jam, was the usual meal. Teenagers like myself were always hungry. Alas, when we needed food most it sometimes did not arrive at all. It was not pleasant to spend twenty-four hours or more in the front line with nothing to eat. Sometimes, when drinking water did not arrive, we had to boil water from shell holes and this may account for the crop of boils and diarrhea that plagued us.

🦴 DID YOU KNOW . . . ? 🦴

French peasants sometimes give rooms to British soldiers and they are glad of Brit biscuits . . . they make great fire-lighters!

Sweet treat

Apart from the bully beef and the Maconochie, the soldiers have two other big moans.

One is the cakes that friends and family send from home! They are deadlier than a German bullet, some soldiers reckon. The other pet hate is explained in this popular 1916 poem.

FEAR

A terror hangs over our heads,
I scarcely dare to think
Of the awful doom that each one dreads
From which the bravest shrink.
It's not the crashing shrapnel shell
It's not the sniper's shot,
It's not the machine gun's burst of Hell,
These matter not a jot.
It's a far worse thing than that, son,
With which we have to grapple.
It's if we see another one
More tin of Plum and Apple

✥ DID YOU KNOW . . . ? ✥

Plum and apple jam arrives in the trenches in tins. At least the empty tins will make useful homemade grenades!

• Fill a jam tin with a high explosive such as gun cotton, or TNT, and pack it with stones or metal scrap.

• Stick in a fuse.

• Light the fuse with a match.

• The jam tin grenade is then hurled at the enemy in a bowling action — 25 to 30 metres is usual.

TAKE THAT!

ER.., I THINK YOU'VE JUST THROWN JAM AT THEM

POOR DEVILS

Food facts

To live in the trenches you need to know the right words so you don't eat your baby's head with pozzy!

NAME	WHAT IT IS
BABY'S HEAD	Meat pudding. It is the shape of a baby's head.
BOMBARDIER	Potatoes. From the French, "pommes de terre."
BURGOO	Porridge. From Arab/Turkish/Hindustani "burghul," an oat porridge.
CHAR	Tea. From Hindustani "char" or Chinese "ch'a."
CHERB	Beer. From Hindustani.
DOG AND MAGGOT	Bread and cheese.
GUNFIRE	Strong tea, usually with rum.
HARD TACK	British army biscuit, eaten cold, usually with bully beef.
JIPPO JUICE	Gravy, usually of bacon. Very popular. Also the shout given by army cooks to call the men to their meals.
JAPAN	Bread. From the French word "pain."
MUCKIM	Butter. From Hindustani.

PARNEE Water. From Hindustani.

PLONK Wine. From French "vin blanc," white wine.

POZZY Jam. Usually tinned plum and apple. Later other mixes like gooseberry and rhubarb will be served.

RUM JAR A drink, but "rum jar" is also the name given to a German mortar bomb, because it's the shape of a rum jar. Don't mix them up! Rum is given to troops in stone jars stamped with the letters S.R.D for Supply Reserve Depot — soldiers say it stands for Soon Runs Dry.

SHACKLES Soup made from leftovers.

SKILLY Watery stew.

SPOTTED DOG Currant pudding.

TICKLER'S Jam, pozzy. From the name of a company in Hull that makes it. The empty tins can be turned into hand grenades, packed with nails, glass and explosives.

TOMMY COOKER A small cooker you can carry around.

WAD Sandwich.

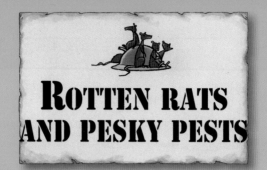

ROTTEN RATS AND PESKY PESTS

Soldiers have more to fear than enemy weapons. Creepy-crawlies and deadly diseases can kill you just as dead.

The average Brit soldier has 20 lice crawling over his body. But what is the record?

10,428[3]

Lovely lice

At the Gallipoli battles in Turkey in 1915, the soldiers are forced to wear the same clothes for weeks without even taking them off. One Australian soldier finally gets to take his socks off and sees a ghastly sight :

> And Ma, I swear that as I dropped my socks on the floor I saw them start to move. They were a seething mass of lice!

In the trenches the soldiers can be found "chatting" to pass the quiet times. But "chatting" doesn't mean talking. It means getting rid of the "chats" or lice from the seams of their tunics.

3 Illustrator note: I've drawn about 100 lice here; couldn't be bothered with the other 10,328!

One soldier compares lice to an army that invaded his body . . .

The Little Soldiers of the Night

Though some hundreds you may kill,
You'll find there's hundreds still,
For they hide beneath each other
And are smart at taking cover;
Then you have an awful bite,
They've a shocking appetite.

There are families in dozens,
Uncles, mothers, sisters, cousins,
And they have their married quarters
Where they rear their sons and daughters;
And they take a lot of catching,
Cause an awful lot of scratching.

Fierce flies

When the British and their Allies fight at Gallipoli in 1915, the flies in the summer are extra bad because of the number of unburied bodies.

One soldier of the Australia and New Zealand Army Corps (Anzacs) writes home about the flies . . .

Some of them must have tin openers on their feet, they bite so hard.

A Brit soldier complains . . .

> In order to eat your food you had to wave your hand over it then bite suddenly, otherwise a fly came with it. Any bit of food uncovered was blotted out of sight by flies in a couple of seconds.

That fly has probably had a picnic on a dead donkey a few minutes before, so it's no wonder the troops suffer so much disease in Gallipoli.

The gory glory of war
One of the most famous victims of the War is the poet Rupert Brooke. He writes a poem about the glory of war before he is sent off. (This is a dumb thing to do since he'd never seen the horror of it, but the people back in Britain want to believe it.)

If I should die, think only this of me:
That there's some corner of a foreign field
That is forever England.

THIS ONE'S FULL UP

He is sent off to fight in Gallipoli but never makes it. In April 1915 he is bitten on the lip by an insect and dies of blood poisoning.

This is probably not the glorious end Rupert imagined. The "corner of a foreign field that is forever England" is his grave in an olive grove on the Greek island of Skyros, by the way.

Rotten rats

Rats enjoy the Frightful First World War . . . mostly. Trenches are overrun with them — there is always plenty to eat, from human food scraps to human corpses.

But most soldiers hate the robbing rodents and spend a lot of their spare time trying to massacre the creepy creatures. Apart from shooting them in the open they also try some sneaky tricks. The following have all been tried in the trenches with great success . . .

VANQUISH VILE VERMIN!

Spade Splat [Method 1]

If rats have been at your bread then place the ruined loaves on the floor of your dugout.

Find yourself a spade and flashlight. Switch off the light.

When you hear the rats swarming over the bread then switch on the flashlight and smash the rats to a pulp.

Cheesy Trick [Method 2]

Put a bayonet on the end of your rifle.

Put a piece of cheese on the end of the bayonet.

Point it towards the enemy lines.

When a rat begins to nibble at the cheese, pull the trigger.

You can't miss!

Smoke 'Em Out [Method 3]

Place cordite at the entrance to rat holes and light it.

The smoke will drive out the rats.

Wait by the exit and smash them with wooden clubs.

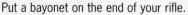

Cordite is used as an explosive to fire shells from guns. A group of Australian soldiers were getting rid of rats this way until the cordite came in contact with an unexploded German bomb. Twenty men were injured . . . but at least the rats were probably pulped!

Terrible terrier-ist
Terrier dogs are useful for killing rats in the trenches. A devoted soldier wrote a poem to his dog, Jim . . .

Jim

A tough little, rough little beggar,
And merry the eyes on him.
But no German or Turk
Can do dirtier work
With an enemy rat than Jim.

And when the light's done and night's falling,
And shadows are darkling and dim,
In my coat you will nuzzle
Your pink little muzzle
And growl in your dreams, little Jim.

There is no record of what the rats thought of little Jim.

Of course not every company in the trenches has a rat-catcher like Jim. What do these poor soldiers do?

They tame the rats and keep them as pets instead!

TRENCH ENTERTAINMENT

Don't think the War is all misery. Troops like to have fun even under fire. They have their own jokes, songs, games and poems to keep them cheerful.

Barge boating

In 1917, as Sergeant Ernest Parker is sitting reading at the entrance to his dugout in the banks of the Yser Canal, he sees an exciting water sport. He reports . . .

A RUFFIAN-LOOKING MEMBER OF MY BAND WAS USING TWO OARS TO ROW A RECTANGULAR BOX UP AND DOWN THE CANAL. HE PUT DOWN THE OARS AND PICKED UP A SHOVEL. WHEN A RIVAL CRAFT WAS LAUNCHED, A NAVAL BATTLE BEGAN, CHEERED BY THE SPECTATORS, WHO WERE HOPING THAT SOMEBODY WOULD TAKE A PLUNGE INTO THE BLACK SLIME OF THE CANAL.

Learn the lingo

Every soldier needs to talk soldier language. Learn these and your sergeant will test you on them tomorrow!

ALLEY	Go! Clear out! Run away! From French "allez."
BUMF	Toilet paper, or newspaper used for the toilet. Later on it came to mean any useless letters from the army. From bum-fodder, a 1700s word.
CANTEEN MEDALS	Beer or food stains on the front of your tunic.
CHARPOY	Bed. From the Hindustani word.
CHAT	A louse.
CHINSTRAPPED	Tired, exhausted. The idea is a man can be so tired he is held upright only by the chinstrap of his cap or helmet. (It's a joke.) In fact, chinstraps are used only by troops on horseback. Other soldiers think that if a bullet hits their helmet, the chinstrap may choke them or break their jaw.
COLD MEAT TICKET	A disc worn around the neck. Men are given red and green discs. These give the name and number of the soldier. If he is killed, one disc stays with the body (the cold meat).
DAISIES	Boots. From Cockney rhyming slang "daisy roots."
DEVIL DODGER	Army priest.
FLEABAG	Sleeping bag.

34

GOGGLE-EYED BOOGER WITH THE TIT	British gas helmet. The wearer has to breathe in through his nose and breathe out through a valve held in his teeth.
JAKES	Latrines. Expression dating back to Elizabethan times.
KILTIE	A Scottish soldier.
KNUT	A person (usually an officer) who is fussy about how they look. The word comes from the popular music-hall song by Arthur Wimperis (1874-1953) Gilbert the Filbert, the Colonel of the Knuts.
LANDOWNER	A dead man. To "become a landowner" was to be dead and buried.
QUICK FIRER	A postcard. The card has sentences printed which can be crossed out to give your message. E.g. "I am/am not fit/dead and, hope to be home soon/next year/in a box."
RATS AFTER MOULDY CHEESE (RAMC)	Doctors and nurses . . . the Royal Army Medical Corps.
REST CAMP	A cemetery.
THIRD MAN	To go too far into danger. This is from a story that an enemy sniper can see a match struck at night. Light a second man's cigarette after your own and the sniper has time to take aim . . . light the third man's and the sniper fires. The second man is fine – the third man is one too far.

35

Why worry?
This is a joke notice that is passed around the trenches.

> ## Don't worry
>
> When you are a soldier you can be in one of two places:
> A dangerous place or a safe place.
> If you're in a safe place . . . don't worry.
> If you're in a dangerous place you can be one of two things:
> One is wounded and the other is not.
> If you're not wounded . . . don't worry.
> If you are wounded it is dangerous or slight.
> If it's slight . . . don't worry.
> If it's dangerous then one of two things will happen:
> You'll die or you'll recover.
> If you recover . . . don't worry.
> If you die . . . you can't worry.
> In these circumstances a soldier never worries.

Silly songs
Soldiers are fond of singing. When they can't find the right song they take a popular one and change the words. In 1914 they are singing . . .

> *Though your heart may ache a while . . . never mind.*
> *Though your face may lose its smile . . . never mind.*
> *For there's sunshine after rain*
> *And then gladness follows pain,*
> *You'll be happy once again . . . never mind.*

The words are soon replaced by more bitter ones . . .

If you're hung up on barbed wire . . . never mind.
      Or . . .
If your sleeping place is damp . . . never mind.
If you wake up with a cramp . . . never mind.
If your trench should fall in some.
Fill your ears and make you dumb
While the sergeant drinks your rum . . . never mind.

Even religious songs are made fun of. A popular one, "What a friend we have in Jesus," becomes . . .

When this lousy war is over,
Oh how happy I will be,
When I get my civvy clothes on,
No more soldiering for me.
No more church parades on Sunday,
No more putting in for leave.
I will kiss the sergeant major,
How I'll miss him, how I'll grieve.

But the song that sums up the War the best is the simplest one of all. It is sung to the tune of "Auld Lang Syne" (the one drunken parents join hands to sing on New Year's).

We're here because we're here because
We're here because we're here.
We're here because we're here because
We're here because we're here.

PAINFUL PUNISHMENTS

Soldiers have to obey rules. Some are simple rules.

SOME BRITISH ARMY RULES

YOU MUST NOT:

- Attack another British soldier
- Give the enemy secret passwords
- Be drunk when on guard
- Pretend to be ill
- Be cruel to a horse
- Insult the King

Break those rules and you could get:

FIELD PUNISHMENT NO. 1

The soldier is tied to a gun wheel by his wrists and ankles for one hour in the morning and one hour in the evening for up to 21 days.

NOT WHILE IT'S BEING USED I HOPE

Dealing death

Some rules can be punished by death if you break them.

> ## SOME BRITISH ARMY SERIOUS RULES
>
> ### YOU MUST NOT:
>
> - **Run away from the army (desert)**
> - **Tell your officer to surrender**
> - **Throw away your weapons**
> - **Help the enemy**
> - **Write or speak to the enemy**
> - **Act like a coward in front of the enemy.**

Break these rules and you could be shot by a firing squad made up of your own troops.

You may be asked to shoot a British soldier if he is a coward. Could you do it? Here is how a French man saw two soldiers executed . . .

THE VICTIMS WERE TIED UP FROM HEAD TO TOE LIKE SAUSAGES. A THICK BANDAGE HID THEIR FACES. AND, A HORRIBLE THING ON THEIR CHESTS WAS A SQUARE OVER THEIR HEARTS. THEY COULD NOT MOVE. THEY HAD TO BE CARRIED LIKE TWO DUMMIES ON THE LORRY, WHICH TOOK THEM TO THE RIFLE RANGE

THE PRIEST MUMBLED SOME WORDS AND THEN WENT OFF TO HIS BREAKFAST. TWO TROOPS OF SIX SOLDIERS APPEARED. THEY LINED UP WITH THEIR BACKS TO THE FIRING POSTS. THE GUNS LAY ON THE GROUND. THE VICTIMS WERE TIED TO THE POSTS

THE TROOPS PICKED UP THEIR GUNS, TURNED ROUND QUICKLY, AIMED AND OPENED FIRE. THEN TURNED THEIR BACKS ON THE BODIES AND THE SERGEANT ORDERED "QUICK MARCH"

THE MEN MARCHED RIGHT PAST THEM WITHOUT TURNING A HEAD. NO PARADE, NO MUSIC. A HIDEOUS DEATH WITHOUT DRUMS OR TRUMPETS

Vilest victims
• Private Thomas Highgate is the first to suffer such a death. During the Battle of Mons, he runs away and hides in a barn. Private Highgate is executed at the age of 17.
• Sixteen-year-old Herbert Burden is shot for running away after seeing his friends massacred at the battlefield of Bellwarde Ridge.

• James Crozier from Belfast is shot at dawn for deserting — he is just 16. Before his execution, Crozier is given so much rum that he passes out. He has to be carried to his execution.
• Private Abe Bevistein, aged 16, is also shot by firing squad at Labourse, near Calais. Just before his trial Bevistein writes home to his mother:

> We were in the trenches. I was so cold I went out (and took shelter in a farm house). They took me to prison so I will have to go in front of the court. I will try my best to get out of it, so don't worry

After a shooting, the doctor will look at the man. If he is still alive, the officer in charge will finish him off with a revolver.

During the First World War, 306 British and Commonwealth soldiers are executed.

✂ DID YOU KNOW . . . ? ✂

Not every victim gets a trial. There is a group of "Battle Police" who follow the army when it attacks. If they catch a soldier hanging back or refusing to go forward they'll arrest him . . . and sometimes just shoot him on the spot.

WICKED WEAPONS II
BIGGER BANGS

The British army needs big guns as well as foot soldiers — the troops of gunners are the "artillery."

Shell-spotter's guide

You need to know what you are firing and what is being fired at you. What would you do with a Blind Pig? Duck or fire it? Learn these different names for shells and what each of them do . . .

1. BLIND PIG Mortar bomb. A mortar is a bomb you pop down a tube to fire and point at the enemy — it is hard to aim it and it doesn't travel a long way but it loops up and lands on top of him then explodes. Nasty.

2. FLYING PIG British 9.45 inch trench mortar bomb.

3. RUM JAR Mortar bomb, the same shape as a rum jar

4. TOFFEE APPLE A mortar bomb on a stick — not so tasty as an apple.

5. GRASS-CUTTERS Small bombs dropped from aircraft on to camps and tents behind the lines. They burst when they land and scatter small steel balls to smash the legs of soldiers in camp . . . or their heads if they are lying asleep.

Tanks

These machines can move forward through mud. The soldiers on foot can walk behind and shelter from enemy bullets.

For: Good shields. Scare the enemy who often run away when they see them.

Against: They break down, and get stuck in the mud. Worst of all is if you're trapped inside when they catch fire.

> **🎀 DID YOU KNOW . . . ? 🎀**
> A tank might also be called a . . .

LAND CREEPER

LAND SHIP

WIBBLE-WOBBLE

BOOJUM

WHIPPET

Oddest of all, the first tank was called "Little Willie" so some soldiers called their tanks "Willies."

AS FAR AS WE KNOW THE GERMANS DO NOT HAVE LITTLE WILLIES. IT'S PROBABLE THEY DON'T HAVE WILLIES AT ALL...

LITTLE WILLIE

SO WHEN THEY SEE ALL OUR WILLIES THEY WILL BE VERY SURPRISED

Dummy tanks

If you want to scare the enemy then make him think you have a tough tank . . . even though you haven't. Make a dummy tank!

There are at least two different types of wooden dummy tanks used in the First World War.

Crews push them around but can't always see where they are going. So some "tanks" have taken their crew over cliffs. Others have made good firewood!

Message rocket

If you're in the trenches and want to send a message you don't want to be cycling or running through gunfire.
Send a message in a rocket.

The rocket has fins that you can twist. They can send the rocket 800 to 2,000 metres in the air.

Try not to hit the general.

MESSAGE FOR YOU SIR

SOLDIER SURVIVAL

If you are hurt, killed or missing you are known as a "casualty." On the first day of the Battle of the Somme, 1 July 1916, there were 58,000 British casualties — about 20,000 of them were dead. The living needed the army hospitals . . .

Fabulous first aid

In the middle of a battle you can't pop down to the local pharmacy for an aspirin or dial 911 for an ambulance. Soldiers have to look after each other and they all carry a small first-aid pack into battle. Brit soldiers also have a book that offers some help.

Don't follow these instructions next time you are flattened in a fierce football match . . .

THE BRITISH ARMY FIELD ALMANAC (1915)

BROKEN LIMBS:

Gently put the broken limb straight after cutting off the clothes. Then fix it in this position by means of a splint made from a rifle, a roll of newspapers, bayonets, swords, pieces of wood.

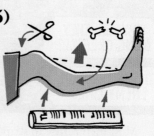

A roll of newspapers! In a battle? What newspaper could be as tough as a wooden splint? *The Daily Telegraph-pole* perhaps?

F-f-f-f-frostbite

Frostbite in the trenches can make your toes drop off.

In winter 1914-15, "anti-frostbite grease" is sent to soldiers in 1-kg tins. It looks like lard and is mostly pork fat.

After 1915 the grease is made from whale oil, sent out in rum jars. Soldiers don't like it because of the terrible smell.

Army orders say . . .

Most men refuse to strip . . . and most officers refuse to rub!

You may not want to suffer the 1915 cure . . .

FROSTBITE:

Carry the sufferer to a room or place without a fire, remove the clothes and rub hard with a cloth soaked in water or snow.

☠ DID YOU KNOW . . . ? ☠

Soldiers who want to look poorly and escape a battle can chew cordite (an explosive) taken from their rifle bullets. Cordite gives the soldier a high temperature but beware, it only works for a short while.

Deadly doctors

Army hospitals in the First World War are better than they were in the Crimean War (1854–6). Nurse Florence Nightingale made things a little safer. Back in Florrie Nightie's day a wound could get infected — if the bullet didn't kill you then the germs did.

But even in the First World War doctors can still be pretty clumsy. One soldier reports . . .

An Australian soldier, Private O'Connor, was wounded in the leg and captured. He was taken to Istanbul where an Armenian doctor operated to cut off O'Connor's leg. The doctor sawed halfway through the bone, grew too tired, and snapped off the rest.

Shocking treatment

Not all illness can be cured in this war. Illness of the mind will not be treated well.

Soldiers can suffer terribly from the endless blast of shells. They suffer "shell shock." In the First World War no one feels very sorry for these poor men. The army says . . .

Some shell-shock victims sometimes run from a battle. Their "treatment" is to be shot by their own army.

SURVIVAL TEST

Will you survive the War? Try this test to see what you know. Just answer True or False . . .

1. Army horses wear gas masks.

2. Lieutenant Henry Webber, a 67-year-old British soldier, is the oldest Brit soldier to die at the Somme.

3. A messenger pigeon is eaten by hungry soldiers.

4. Troops are served dinner by French waitresses.

5. A tiny steel helmet is made for a pet dog.

6. A trench is built in the shape of the Tower of London.

7. Bricks are dropped by German Zeppelin flyers.

8. Goldfish are used to test for poison gas.

9. Grenades are hit towards German trenches with cricket bats.

10. Horse poo is burned on camp fires.

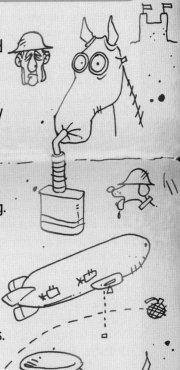

Answers:

1 True. They are made specially to fit horses because horses are nearly as important as soldiers.

2 True. And the youngest Brit soldier to die in the War was 14-year-old Private John Condon of the Royal Irish Regiment. He died in battle on 24 May 1915.

3 True. Pigeon pie is very tasty and if there are no messages to send you may as well eat one. It's not pie in the sky — and it's not pigeon in the sky either.

4 False. There are tales that Brit soldiers are living a good life in France. They are NOT true. Soldiers eat awful meals and never get to see a French waitress.

5 True. Soldiers don't fight ALL the time. In the quiet hours they have time to make things, like a helmet for their pet pooch.

6 False. Trenches are built in the best place you can find. There is no time for fancy stuff.

7. True. A brick dropped from half a mile can do a lot of damage to your head. Zeppelin flyers also drop steel darts. They REALLY part your hair.

8 True. Your gas mask may smell clean, but you need to check. Pour water through it into a goldfish bowl. If the fish flips and flops dead then don't use the gas mask. About a million men will die from gas attacks in the War.

9 False. But Australian soldiers did have a grenade they threw at the Germans that they called a "Cricket Bat." What a wicket idea, eh?

10 False. But they DO let horse poo stew till it gives off a gas. The gas is then used to make gas fires in the trenches. Cosy.

SOLDIER SPIRITS

A lot of people die in war so it's not surprising there are a lot of ghost stories . . .

The angel army of Mons

In August 1914 British troops arrive in Belgium to try and stop the German invaders. They are beaten back and slaughtered by the enemy.

Over 15,000 die in the early attacks. Yet some survive and reports say this is thanks to a miracle . . .

WE SAW OUR ST GEORGE LEADING A TROOP OF PHANTOM FIGHTERS ON HORSEBACK. THEY DROVE THE GERMANS BACK

OUI, MON AMI, BUT IT WAS OUR JOAN OF ARC NOT ST. GEORGE WHO CAME TO OUR RESCUE

WHATEVER

Arthur Machen, a journalist, turns the rumours into a short story. His story (called *The Bowmen*) says it was the English heroes of the 1415 Battle of Agincourt who had come to the rescue. (That battle was fought nearby.)

Machen's story is published in the *London Evening News* a few weeks after the Battle of Mons and many Brits believe it. Some of the soldiers returning from the battle say it is true.

Even when Machen says he invented the whole story there are some people who go on believing in the angels.

The spirit of the Somme
Soldiers in hospital enjoy swapping stories . . . some are strange and mysterious.

WE HAD A CAPTAIN IN THE BATTLE OF THE SOMME. A TALL HANDSOME BLOKE AND A FINE LEADER. ONE DAY SOME CHAPS GOT THEMSELVES TRAPPED IN A SHELL HOLE. HE FOUND THEM AND LED THEM TO SAFETY. THEY WAS TERRIFIED, BUT HE SAID...

DON'T BE FRIGHTENED, MEN – WHENEVER YOU GET YOURSELF INTO A TIGHT CORNER I'LL BE THERE TO PULL YOU OUT

AND HE WAS THERE FOR US, TIME AND AGAIN. BUT HE DID IT ONCE TOO OFTEN. HE GOT HIMSELF KILLED HELPING SOME CHAPS AT THE SOMME. WE CRIED FOR HIM LIKE A BROTHER. I TOOK OVER AS PLATOON COMMANDER AND I GOT OUR LADS INTO A RIGHT FIX AT ALBERT. WE WAS DOOMED! THEN I TURN ROUND AND I SEES THE CAPTAIN WITH HIS BRIGHT EYES AND HIS CHEERFUL SMILE

WELL, WILLIS, IT'S BEEN A CLOSE SHAVE THIS TIME, BUT I THINK WE'LL PULL IT OFF IF YOU FOLLOW ME

SO I LEADS THE MEN THE WAY THE CAPTAIN SHOWS ME. AND, BLOW ME, NO SOONER ARE WE SAFE THAN HE DISAPPEARS! WHAT DO YOU MAKE OF THAT?

PART II: GERMANY KNOW YOUR ENEMY

You are fighting for THE CENTRAL POWERS, Germany and Austria-Hungary, Turkey and Bulgaria.

You are fighting against THE ALLIES ... The Enemy! That's Britain and the British Empire, France, Belgium, Russia, Italy and Serbia (the USA, China, Greece, Portugal, Japan and Romania will join in later).

28 June 1914. The evil Serbians have murdered our friend, the heir to the Austrian Empire, Archduke Franz Ferdinand. Austria declares war on Serbia and we Germans help Austria ...

... so Russia helps Serbia, so France helps Russia. Germany marches through Belgium to get to France, so Britain helps Belgium.

We tell the German people stories so they hate the British and love the German Army. What we say may not be true ... but believe it anyway. Read these stories and learn to hate!

1 If the British capture a German soldier they'll gouge out his eyes!

2 French gold is being taken in cars through Germany to Russia to help the war against us. Let's wreck all foreign cars!

3 We didn't start this war. It was France, not Germany, that marched though Belgium to attack us! And when we meet a friend in the street we no longer say, "Guten Morgen" (good morning), we say, "Gott strafe England" (God punish England).
"Gott strafe England" is rubber-stamped on letters, printed on millions of postcards, engraved on badges and brooches.

When you go to war you can't fight against nice people, can you? You have to believe the enemy are real slime-balls who would murder your granny and poison your gerbil if they won. You have to learn to hate them.

This song is written in 1914 when the War starts. It is known as "The Song of Hate" (or *"Hasslied"* in German.) German soldiers can sing it as they march into battle. It says the French and Russian enemies don't matter — there is just one REAL enemy we all have to hate . . .

The Hasslied

French and Russian, they matter not,
A blow for a blow, a shot for a shot,
We fight the battle with bronze and steel,
And the time that is coming peace will seal.
You we will hate with a lasting hate,
We will never give up our hate,
Hate by water and hate by land,
Hate of the head and hate of the hand,
Hate of the hammer and hate of the crown,
Hate of seventy millions choking down.
We love as one, we hate as one,
We have one enemy, one alone . . .
ENGLAND!

Of course one of the deadliest fellers is the one who plans the battles and sends you to fight them. Your OWN leader!

56

PUBLIC ENEMY NUMBER 1

Kaiser Wilhelm

Job: Emperor (or Kaiser) of Germany

Nickname: William. Wilhelm's mum was the daughter of British Queen Victoria — so she calls her son the British name William . . . but the Germans call him Wilhelm. So he is a bit mixed up. Woeful Willy. When war starts he enjoys his title "Supreme War Lord."

Peculiarity: Unpopular. Nobody likes poor Willy. His grandmother, Queen Victoria, can't stand him. His mother beat him and refused to wish him a happy birthday . . . so he sulks for days. His father thought he would be a dangerous leader — smart Dad!

Weakness: He was born with a withered left arm and it embarrasses him. When he is photographed he insists that he hides his weak arm. People around him hide their strong left arms too.

Nasty streak: German workers go on strike and he orders soldiers to attack them. "I expect my troops to shoot at least 500," he said.

Most likely to say: "The English are mad, mad, mad as March hares."

Least likely to say: "I am mad, mad, mad as a March hare!"

CURIOUS CLOTHING

Everyone needs a uniform. The German uniform is just so much better than the British . . .

HOT HELMET

At the start of the War the German soldiers have a flashy helmet called the *pickelhaube*, which of course means "pointy hat." Because it's a hat with a point.

The *pickelhaube* was dreamed up in 1842 by King Frederick William IV of Prussia. He thought of putting the spike on top. Can you see the point?

The helmets are made of leather painted shiny black. Soldiers usually hate wearing them because they fall off easily.

When war starts the Germans discover something terrible . . . leather *pickelhaubes* don't stop bullets. In 1915 the Germans start making steel helmets – the job of making them goes to factories that used to make pots and pans.

In February 1916, the Stahlhelm (steel helmet) is given to soldiers. This saves a lot of lives. But *pickelhaube* helmets are still worn by some soldiers in 1917.

GOD'S BELT

Each side believes that they are in the right; that of course God is on their side.

So you go to war with a belt buckle that reads *Gott mitt uns*. For British readers, that means "God with us." And, of course, he is.

COOL COATS

The winter of 1914–15 is really cold and wet. Trenches flood and men suffer "trench foot" . . . it can mean having your legs cut off to save your life. It helps if you rub smelly whale oil into your feet. Or wear boots up to your thighs – like fishermen. And you need a long, warm coat. Germans are given 'greatcoats' which are simply great! The British even go out into no man's land to steal German greatcoats from enemy corpses.

A Brit soldier called Robert Graves was collecting coats one day to keep his men warm. Suddenly he came across a rotting German corpse – the greatcoat hadn't saved that German. Graves went on to write a poem about the horrible sight . . .

> *. . . propped against a shattered trunk,*
> *In a great mess of things unclean,*
> *Sat a dead Boche[4] he scowled and stunk*
> *With clothes and face a sodden green,*
> *Big-bellied, spectacled, crop-haired,*
> *Dribbling black blood from nose and beard*

Graves didn't steal that mouldy coat!

4 Boche was the nasty name Brit soldiers gave to their German enemies.

BARMY BATTLE PLANS

Simple Schlieffen

Germany is ready for war in 1914. They already have a plan: the Schlieffen plan. It is simple as ABC . . .

It goes wrong for three reasons . . .

• Belgium puts up a fight and that gives Britain time to send troops across to help France.

• Russia rushes to get its army ready and attacks from the east while France and Britain fight in the west.

• Machine guns and trenches stop both armies dead.

Schlieffen wanted a six-week sprint. Trenches turn it into a four-year muddy marathon.

Battle plan

Now that the enemies are frozen face-to-face in their trenches the Germans need a new battle plan . . .

THERE WILL BE JUST A FEW GAPS IN THE BARBED WIRE. AIM YOUR MACHINE GUNS AT THE GAPS AND CUT THEM DOWN. EASY!

GAP IN WIRE

Soldier statues

Sounds simple. In fact the shelling terrifies German troops even in their dugouts. German soldier Wilhelm Hermanns writes about the soldiers who come out of their hiding places covered in concrete dust. It is a scary sight.

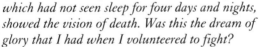

There were about 20 men. They walked like living plaster statues. Their faces stared at us like those of shrunken mummies, and their eyes seemed so huge that one saw nothing but eyes. Those eyes, which had not seen sleep for four days and nights, showed the vision of death. Was this the dream of glory that I had when I volunteered to fight?

WICKED WEAPONS

Here are some of the weapons you may be asked to use against the enemy . . .

SAW-BACK BAYONET

A dagger that fits on the end of your Gewehr 98 rifle and can be used to stab the enemy. Rule books say, "Aim the bayonet at the throat, breast or groin."
For: The saw-back means it can be used to cut wood. It can also be taken out and used as a dagger.
Against: The enemy believe we are animals who use it to saw off their heads. (We don't . . . but we could if we wanted to!)

STICK GRENADE

A little bomb with a handle (the stick). Pull out the pin then throw it. It goes off after seven seconds.
For: Throw one into an enemy trench and kill several men with one bomb. You can carry quite a few in a bag around your neck.
Against: Time it wrong and they may throw it back. Or the stick might snap and the bomb fall at your feet.

FLAMMENWERFER

Small flamethrower carried by a single man. A gas bottle on the back throws out a stream of burning oil up to 18 metres.

For: Brings terror to the Brits in Flanders 1915. Blinds and scorches the enemy.

Against: Can explode and blow a hole in your back. Enemy soldiers aim at you because you scare them. Don't expect to live long.

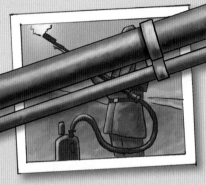

BERGMANN MP18 SUBMACHINE GUN

By 1918 we Germans have one-man machine guns that are light enough to be carried into battle.

For: The guns are just 9–14 kg — not much heavier than a rifle but they fire 32 bullets in a burst.

Against: The gun is light but the drums of 32 bullets are heavy. They fasten to the side of the gun and make it hard to hold and aim. A hard knock can make the gun go off by itself and spray your friends with lead.

GERMAN GRANATENWERFER MORTAR BOMBS

Fired from German trenches into enemy trenches. The early ones are called *Priesterwerfer* (Priest-thrower) because they were invented by a Hungarian priest and can be fired from a rifle. The British call them "pineapples."

For: The shell sends splinters of metal through the air when it explodes and rips the enemy apart. Some can travel 300 metres to the target and a soldier can fire up to 300 of them in an hour. Some can also be used to fire messages to friends. (These don't explode!)

Against: It whistles as it flies so the enemy gets a warning. If it is fired less than 50 metres it can kill your own troops. Less than 20 metres and it will kill you!

TERRIBLE TOILETS

Soldiers need toilets the same as the people back home. The trouble is they don't have nice comfy ones like you!

Terrible toilets

What does a German soldier do when he is not in the trenches — the "front line?" What would you do to relax? Sleep? Write letters to your family? Clean your toenails? No. You'd go to the toilet for a chat.

ONE DAY IN THE TRENCHES...

HI CARL! BUSY?

ME? NO, NOT REALLY

FANCY A POO?

OOOH LOVELY

Toilets are built just behind the trenches out of sight of the enemy. They are usually deep pits with wooden seats on top. When the pit is full it is closed and another one dug.

Erich Maria Remarque is the author of the famous War book, *All Quiet on the Western Front*. He says . . .

The older soldiers don't use the unpleasant, indoor, common toilet, where 20 men sit side-by-side in a line. As it is not raining, they use the individual square wooden boxes with carrying handles on the sides. They pull three into a circle and sit there in the sun all afternoon, reading, smoking, talking, playing cards.

Dreadful disease

Germans try hard to keep their trenches as clean as possible. Dirty toilets can give you a disease called dysentry.

That means . . .

- pain in the guts
- painful pooing
- bloody poo
- sickness
- fever
- possible death

🕱 DID YOU KNOW . . . ? 🕱

A soldier usually makes over a kilogram of poo and pee each day.
In an army company in the trenches this is a ton a week.

FOUL FOOD

By March 1916 Germany is running out of food. German soldiers are told to have one day a week without food to save on supplies . . . but the officers seem to eat well every day!

Belly laughs

The British people believe that the Germans will be starved into defeat. In 1914 Germany only produces 80 percent of its food, 20 percent has to be brought from other countries. If the British Navy can block food ships going to Germany, the army and people will suffer and grow weak.

In September 1915 the Germans can still laugh about the British Navy. That month a Zeppelin raid on London drops 70 bombs, killing 26 people and wounding almost 100. The crew also drop a ham bone attached to a parachute. On it is written: ⟶

A gift from starved out Germany.

By September 1918 the Germans have stopped laughing . . . and they don't have any spare ham bones for jokes.

Suffering civilians

Soldiers may go hungry from time to time. But the people of Germany are starving for most of the Great War.

As early as 1915, "Eat Less" posters appear all over Germany with the "Ten Food Commandments." These include . . .

> **No7: Do not cut off a slice of bread more than you need to eat. Always think of the soldiers in the field who would love to have the bread which you waste.**

Fake food

Germans don't just suffer from food shortages; they also have to put up with fake or "ersatz" food.

Why not try these tasty treats?

BREAD	made with flour of dried beans and peas . . . often sawdust was added
CAKES	made from clover and chestnut flour
LAMB CHOPS	made from rice
STEAK	pale green, made from spinach, spuds, ground nuts and fake eggs

BUTTER	made from curdled milk, sugar and yellow colouring
EGGS	made from a mix of maize and potatoes
PEPPER	has ashes added to make it go further
FATS	from rats, mice, hamsters, crows, cockroaches, snails, worms, hair clippings, old leather boots and shoes.
COFFEE	made from roast nuts with coal tar or roasted acorns or beechnuts.

When all the acorns are needed to be fed to pigs, coffee is made from carrots and turnips.

Horse sense

The army gives the soldiers some tips on cooking a tasty meal . . .

> For tender roast horse flesh, you should boil it first in a little water, before you put it in the roasting pan.

But they only eat horses for the mane course.

I DON'T KNOW WHAT'S WORSE, BEING KILLED, COOKED AND CARVED UP – OR THAT JOKE

Tasty trench food

As the War goes on, the food gets less. Here is what a soldier gets at the start of the War and at the end . . .

1914 DAILY FOOD

1 1/2lb (750g) bread

3/4lb (375g) fresh or frozen meat

3 1/4lb (1.5kg) potatoes

3/4oz (25g) coffee

3/4oz (25g) salt

3/4oz (20g) sugar

two cigars and two cigarettes

10ml rum, 250ml wine, 500ml beer

LOVELY

1918 DAILY FOOD

corned beef

biscuits

I'LL PASS

5-7 pints (3-4 l) of army tea

By late 1918, even ersatz foods have run out. For German soldiers struggling to fight, a meal might be turnip stew served with chunks of turnip bread. Nice.

ROTTEN RATS AND PESKY PESTS

Life in the trenches is dirty as well as dangerous. A German painter, Otto Dix, becomes a soldier and writes a letter home . . .

Lice, rats, barbed wire, fleas, shells, bombs, underground caves, corpses, blood, liquor, mice, cats, filth, bullets, fire, steel; that is what war is. It is the work of the devil.

Lousy life

If German soldiers leave food lying around — or even drop crumbs — then rats will rush in.

Horse's stables are popular with rats . . .

BEST PLACE AROUND

I KNOW MY OATS

When the army moves forward it sometimes leaves food dumps behind. A real ratty feast!

Of course rats will run around in no man's land as dead soldiers make a tasty treat. Make sure bodies are always buried as quickly as possible. Seeing your friend being eaten for breakfast by a rat will make any soldier sick.

❧❧ DID YOU KNOW . . . ? ❧❧

German soldiers often keep cats in their trenches, not just to catch rats but because cats also give early warning of a British gas attack. They become restless, as though they can scent the poison gas before the main cloud appears.

Lovely lice

German soldiers have their own way of dealing with their blood-sucking friends. Here's how . . .

FIRST TAKE THE LID FROM A BOOT POLISH TIN

HOLD IT OVER A CANDLE USING A PIECE OF WIRE

WHEN THE LID BEGINS TO GLOW THEN DROP THE LICE ON THE RED-HOT TIN

THE SIZZLE OF THE FRYING LICE IS A SWEET SOUND TO YOUR EARS

TRENCH ENTERTAINMENT

German soldiers like to have fun in their spare time. Here is a good game . . .

BEETLE RACING

1. You need two or more beetles, a table, sugar and some matchsticks

2. Each jockey chooses a beetle and holds it at one end of the table

3. A sugar lump is placed at the other end of the table to attract the beetles

4. Every jockey places one matchstick on the table

5. On a signal the beetles are released. The first beetle to reach the sugar wins and the winning jockey collects everyone else's matchsticks

And the beetles get to eat the sugar. Of course.

Blow football

Of course the Germans are not crazy like some of the British. Brits like Wilfred Nevill who think war is just a sport.

Nevill writes to his sister Else, on June 28, describing the heavy British shelling of the German trenches, which failed to destroy the machine guns. Wilf writes . . .

As I write the shells are fairly hairing over; you know one gets just sort of bemused after a few million, still it'll be a great experience to tell one's children about.

Nevill didn't live long enough to do that. On 1 July 1916, he and another officer kicked two soccer balls into no man's land and headed across to the German trenches.

Nevill was killed instantly, but the story of the soccer balls was reported widely in the press. In Britain it is seen as a show of courage; in Germany it is seen as a show of British madness.

Paper power

Bored? Then why not write a letter to the enemy and see if you can make them shiver with fear. This is an actual letter from a German soldier to the British:

My dear friend Tommy, I am sorry that I cannot speak English very fine and therefore I only wish to say that if you wish to be my friend, you must stop your shelling with your great "Bum bums" and with your guns too, or I shall coming and do make "Irish stew" from your bodies. Have you understand me? I hope you shall find this little letter and bring answer on the same way. From your affectionate German Kamerad.

Free the prisoner (Australian rules)

There are reports of this game really happening, so it is probably true, but extremely rare.

1. You need a grenade and a prisoner.
2. First find a prisoner who wants to go free.
3. Take him to the gates of the prison and place a hand grenade in his back pocket. Pull the pin out of the grenade (which will explode in five seconds).
4. Hold the prisoner for a count of "one-two," then release him and tell him to run.
5. If he gets the grenade out of his pocket in the remaining three seconds he is the winner and is free to go.
6. If he gets the grenade out of his pocket and throws it back at you then you are losers. But that's the risk you take.

PAINFUL PUNISHMENTS

Soldiers who disobey orders must be punished.

Merciful military
In the Great War the British shoot 268 men for deserting their posts. The German records are destroyed but it seems they shoot only 48 of their own men.

The Russians soon give up shooting their own soldiers and the Australians don't shoot any.

Toothbrush torture
The Germans have their own way of dealing with problem soldiers. They are sorted out in the training camps before they go to fight.

Troublemakers in training are given these nice little tasks . . .

• scrub out the Corporals' Room with a toothbrush
• clear the barrack square of snow with hand brushes and dustpans. This is to be done on Sundays (your only day off)
• parade in full uniform with pack and rifle and then practise attacking and lying down in a muddy field until you are exhausted and filthy . . .

- . . . then, four hours later, report with every item of uniform and kit cleaned, even if your hands are bleeding and raw from cleaning them.

Now the good news . . . once you're trained you will be sent to the front. You will be given a pretty bunch of flowers to wear in your belts.

False fable
Many British soldiers believe that German soldiers are tied to their machine guns to stop them from running away. In fact, German machine-gunners wear special belts with which they can carry their machine guns and leave their hands free.

They work in pairs — one to fire, one to load. If both soldiers are killed while carrying their gun, British soldiers may find the bodies "tied" to the guns. But it's NOT a German punishment!

ER ... THAT'S NOT A MACHINE GUN ROLF

WICKED WEAPONS II
BIGGER BANGS

Bertha isn't a woman! She is a massive gun that fires huge shells for many miles.

Big Bertha

Big Bertha is the 420 mm cannon used by German forces as they march through Belgium in 1914. The gun factory that made her is owned by the Krupp family, and their grandmother is called Bertha. Big Bertha the gun is so big she can't be towed to the battlefield — she has to be carried there in pieces on a train and put together again. But in 1918 a new Big Bertha (usually called "The Paris Gun") drops shells on the French capital city of Paris . . . from 43.5 kilometres away!

☠ DID YOU KNOW . . . ? ☠

Big Bertha needs 285 men to fire her and can only fire eight shells an hour.

Name that shell

German shells bring terror as well as death to the British. Learn their names and what they do.

WHITE STAR A mixture of chlorine and phosgene gas. A white star is painted on the shell casing

WHIZZ-BANG A very fast shell. Name comes from the noise of the flight and the explosion

FOUR-TWO 4.2-inch artillery shell

COAL-BOX Heavy shell, usually a 5.9-inch. Name comes from the black smoke of the shell-burst

CRUMP 5.9-inch shell. Name comes from the noise it makes

MINENWERFER A trench mortar

MOANING MINNIE This is the name given by the British to the minenwerfer because of the noise the fired shells make

GREEN CROSS Full of phosgene gas, it lands and gasses you. It has a green cross painted on the shell casing

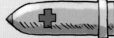

JACK JOHNSON Shell that bursts with black smoke. It's named after the boxer Jack Johnson (1878–1946), the first black American world heavyweight champion (1908–1915)

SILENT SUSAN Very fast shell — it explodes and kills you before you even hear it coming

POTATO MASHER Stick grenade. It looks like a potato masher!

SAUSAGE Mortar bomb

WOOLLY BEAR Explosive shell, bursts with a cloud like a woolly teddy bear

YELLOW CROSS Gas shell. A yellow cross is painted on the shell casing

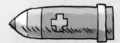

Silly songs

The British make up comic songs about German shells. Songs like, "I want to go home . . ."

I want to go home, I want to go home.
I don't want to go in the trenches no more,
Where whizz-bangs and shrapnel they whistle and roar.
Take me over the sea, where the Germans can't get at me.
Oh my, I don't want to die, I want to go home.

Whizz-bangs are so popular they even have their own song, "Hush, here comes a whizz-bang."

HUSH, HERE COMES A WHIZZ-BANG.
HUSH, HERE COMES A WHIZZ-BANG.
NOW YOU SOLDIER MEN GET DOWN THOSE STAIRS,
DOWN IN YOUR DUGOUTS AND SAY YOUR PRAYERS.
HUSH, HERE COMES A WHIZZ-BANG.
AND IT'S MAKING RIGHT FOR YOU.
AND YOU'LL SEE ALL THE WONDERS OF NO-MAN'S-LAND,
IF A WHIZZ-BANG HITS YOU

Zeppelins

A Zeppelin is a gas-filled balloon with a motor to take it where you want it to go.

On 19 January 1915, the Germans make the first Zeppelin airship raids to drop bombs on Britain — on Great Yarmouth and Kings Lynn on the east coast. On 7 June 1915, the first Zeppelin airship is shot down over Flanders, northern France.

For: Women and children, cats and dogs are in this War, like it or not. If they are attacked they may try to stop the War. On 14 October 1915 five Zeppelins kill 71 in London.

Against: That slow-moving bag of gas makes a Zeppelin an easy target for an enemy fighter plane. And they burn fiercely.

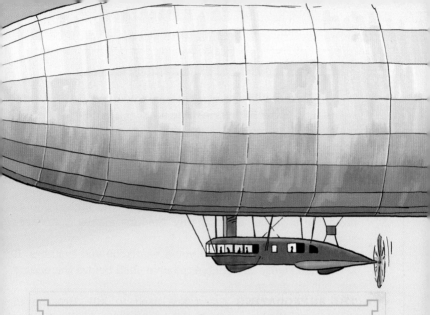

🕸 **DID YOU KNOW . . . ?** 🕸

A Zeppelin is shot down over London and a reporter goes to see where it has crashed in flames. He writes . . .

The crew numbered nineteen. One body was found in the field some way from the wreckage. He must have jumped from the doomed airship from a great height. So great was the force with which he struck the ground that I saw the print of his body clearly in the grass. There was a round hole for the head, then deep marks of the body, with outstretched arms, and finally the legs wide apart. Life was in him when he was picked up, but the spark soon went out. He was, in fact, the commander of the airship.

On 22 April 1915 a nasty new weapon, poisoned gas, is first used against soldiers in the trenches.

Gruesome gases

All gases are nasty but they do different things to the enemy.

THE LACRYMATORS A type of tear gas that makes you go blind for a while. Even a tiny amount makes your eyes sting.

THE STERNUTATORS give you a headache and sickness. It arrives suddenly in a high-explosive shell before the enemy can put on gas masks.

THE SUFFOCATING gases are used to kill. Breathe in these gases and your lungs fill up with liquid. You drown in your own body fluids.

PHOSGENE smells like rotten hay but doesn't make your nose or your eyes itch so you don't know you've breathed it in – till you start to choke to death.

THE VESICANT type of gas. The British call it "mustard gas." It has no smell so the enemy doesn't know it's been gassed until it's too late.

Sing while you're gassing

Of course the British soon have a song about gas shells too.

*GASSED LAST NIGHT, AND GASSED THE NIGHT BEFORE
GOING TO GET GASSED TONIGHT IF WE NEVER
GET GASSED ANYMORE
WHEN WE'RE GASSED, WE'RE SICK AS WE CAN BE
FOR PHOSGENE AND MUSTARD GAS IS MUCH TOO
MUCH FOR ME*

SOLDIER SURVIVAL

War takes its toll on everything and everyone. Just surviving becomes a challenge.

Shell hell

The huge shells that explode during a battle kill and wound hundreds of soldiers. But they do something else. Endless gunfire breaks the minds of some men just as it breaks the bodies of others.

The popular name for the effect is "shell shock" — the medical name is now "Post-Traumatic Stress Disorder." It doesn't matter what you call it really. Men suffer nightmares and fear of loud noises for the rest of their lives.

George Bucher, a German Officer in 1917, explains how the illness affected one young man . . .

After four days of the bombardment a very young soldier had had enough. He climbed out of the trench with two hand grenades from which he had taken the safety pins. He told his comrades what he thought about the War. He was going to run towards the British rifle fire and throw his grenades at them. He threatened to throw them at his comrades if they tried to stop him. They let him go . . .

Of course he is shot down long before he reaches the British trenches. It is suicide and just another of the hundreds of ways to die in this War.

Vile verse

British poets write dozens of famous war poems. The German war poets are often forgotten. But their poems are just as gruesome. Like this story, told by a DEAD German soldier . . .

> *There is a cornfield where black rain falls*
> *There is a brown tree standing lonely here.*
> *There is a hissing wind that haunts the empty huts.*
> *Returning home*
> *The shepherds find my sweet body,*
> *Rotting in the bramble bush.*
> *My ghost is far from gloomy villages,*
> *Spiders look for my heart,*
> *There is a light that fails in my mouth.*
>
> By Georg Trakl

"Spiders look for my heart!" Creepy.

Georg Trakl is a doctor with the German army. He is so upset by the horrors of war he kills himself.

🐀 DID YOU KNOW . . . ? 🐀

By 1918 there is hardly enough cloth left in Germany to make clothes. There isn't even enough for bandages. German soldiers are forced to use bandages made from crepe paper and tie them on with thread.

SURVIVAL TEST

Will you survive the War? Try this test to see what you know. Just answer True or False . . .

1 There are factories for melting down the corpses of horses.

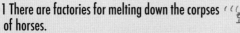

2 Dogs are used to carry secret messages.

3 Dogs are also put in harnesses and used to drag machine guns around the battlefield.

4 Squadrons of hawks and falcons are used to catch any pigeon flying over the English Channel to Britain.

5 German submarines take prisoners.

6 German soldiers catch a nurse helping Brit prisoners to escape. They feel sorry for her and let her go.

7 In 1914 French soldiers are driven off to the trenches in taxis.

8 In 1918-19 more people around the world will die of flu than will die in the whole of the War.

9 One German pilot flies an aeroplane painted bright red so you can't miss him!

10 One of our generals is called Adolf Hitler – the man who will later lead Germany into another great war.

Answers:

1 True. The horse fats are used to make bombs.

2 True. They can be trained to run over the battlefield with messages fastened to their collars. Enemy soldiers watch for messenger dogs and try to turn them into dead dogs.

3 True.

4 True.

5 False. They are too small and have no room for prisoners. Sailors from sunken ships are left to drown.

6 False. Nurse Edith Cavell helps about 200 soldiers to escape before the Germans execute her.

7 True. As German forces march towards Paris on 7 September 1914, the French troops are rushed out using a fleet of Paris taxi cabs — 600 of them carry about 6,000 French troops to the battle. And it works!

8 True. By November 1918 the War has killed about 8.5 million people. But that is nothing to what happens next. "Spanish flu" spreads around the world.

People collapse in the streets, at work and at home. It appears to hit young, healthy people more than the old or very young. The deadly virus attacks the lungs which turn hard, making breathing impossible, until the victim drowns in fluid. At the moment of death, germ-filled fluid pours out of the victim's mouth and nose. By May 1919 Spanish flu has killed over 50,000 in Canada and over 20 million around the world — far more in one year than the War managed in four.

9 True. Baron Manfred von Richthofen shoots down 80 enemy planes before he is finally killed. He wants to bring terror to the enemy so he has a red aeroplane — the enemy can see him coming and are too frightened to fight.

10 False . . . sort of. Adolf Hitler DOES fight in the First World War but he is a humble corporal, not a general. He is wounded but survives . . . sadly.

SOLDIER SPIRITS

British soldiers tell ghost stories and so do the German soldiers. Do ghosts go on fighting in the afterlife? Spooky scrapping and phantom firing?

The German officer

This is a story told by a British soldier about a German ghost . . .

There were three of us on watch that night. That's the way it usually worked. One stood on watch while the other two slept. Then, after a couple of hours, staring into the dark your eyes started to play tricks on you, didn't they? You started seeing Germans running towards you with rifles when there was nothing but rats and corpses out in no man's land.

The German trenches were just 80 yards away from ours that month. You could see their soldiers plain as a pork pie when they stuck their heads above the parapet. After a while you got to know some of them. We didn't really know them . . . I mean we started to give them names . . . the fat one was Hans and the little one with a helmet too large we called Fritz, and so on.

But there was one we knew just as the Kaiser. His back was straight as my rifle and he marched along his trench with no fear of our lads shooting him. There was something about him that made you want to shoot him, know what I mean?

What's the word? Arrogant! He was almost daring us to shoot. There were some crack shots in our company that could have done it too!

Anyway, I was getting to the end of my two hours' watch and it was silent out there. You could hear the rats crunching over the icy soil of no man's land. You could hear other sentries coughing half a mile away. No one could walk along my trench without me hearing.

So imagine my surprise when I turned and saw a man standing there as close to me as the whiskers on my chin. I gave a small cry of shock. He was an officer — he had a long greatcoat on, the sort we pinched from the Germans to keep us warm on frosty nights like this. I stood to attention. "Sorry, sir, didn't see you, sir!"

He was pale-faced in the starlight and there seemed to be a wound on the side of his head. "Are you all right, sir?"

"Yes," he said and gave a sharp nod. "Can you tell me the way to the German trenches, please?" he asked.

Funny sort of question! I stretched out an arm and pointed.
"Due east, sir," I told him.
"Danke," he said.
"What?"
"Thank you," he said and climbed the step to the parapet. Danke? A German word, isn't it?

"You can't go out there without a helmet, sir," I called after him.

His voice floated back as he walked without a sound into the darkness. Rat feet crunched. His didn't. "They won't hurt me. Mein kameraden won't hurt me," he said. And he was gone.

I woke Bert and told him it was his turn to stand guard. "I'm too tired," I said. "I think I'm seeing things."
"What things?"

"I thought I saw a German officer asking the way back to his trenches. I've never seen the Kaiser without his helmet but that bloke sure as hell looked like him."

Bert snorted. "I doubt it, Bill," he laughed. "Has nobody told you?"

"Told me what?"

"That officer we call the Kaiser lost his mind this afternoon — set off walking towards our trenches, firing his pistol."

"We captured him?"

"What? With him firing away like that? Nah. Jimmy Pearce shot him stone dead. We dragged the body into the trench and sent him behind the lines. He's in a British graveyard by now."

I shook my head slowly. "No, Bert, his body may be there . . . but there's some part of him looking for the way back home."

I looked out into the empty dark. The war went on. But one German had found peace.

Somehow I hope he found his way back home.

EPILOGUE

Hungry people lose the will to fight.

The Germans were starved for four years. They lost that will. The Allies, who hadn't suffered nearly so much, did not lose their will.

It's one of the reasons the Germans lost. It was also a reason why the Germans felt so bitter at losing. All that pain for nothing.

Even the people back home had starved and lost their loved ones. Imagine if you were a German parent. The last letter you received from your son said this . . .

> Dear Parents
> I am lying on the battlefield, wounded in the body. I think I am dying. I am glad to have time to prepare for the heavenly home coming
> Thank you dear parents, God be with you.
>
> Johannes

The writer was a German student, 24-year-old Johannes Haas. He died. Germany lost the War. No wonder his parents were among the millions of Germans who wanted revenge.

Ten years after the First World War ended, that bitterness drove them to support a cruel and half-crazed man called Adolf Hitler.

He led them into a another war.

In the Second World War the world had even more vicious weapons to kill far, far more people.

Neither side had learned the lesson. The lesson that says war brings death, destruction and despair. And war has no real winners.

More than ninety years after the First World War ended some people still haven't learned.

INTERESTING INDEX

Hang on! This isn't one of your boring old indexes. This is a horrible index. It's the only index in the world where you will find "blind pigs," "knuckledusters," "toffee apples" and all the other things you really HAVE to know if you want to be a horrible historian. Read it and creep.